Fabrics Work
My Creative Journey

By Edna J. Patterson-Petty

ISBN:1475170637
ISBN-13:9781475170634

Photos: Allied Photo
Cover ©Village Gate, 31 x 25, 2004, owners: Shirley & Harry Portwood

Dedication

This quilt catalog is dedicated to my friend and husband Reginald Petty who by far is my greatest fan. I totally value and respect his opinion as he has always had faith in me, long before I had faith in myself. Through his love and patience I have been free to work relentlessly on my art. When I am too exhausted from creating to prepare dinner, he will go out and get dinner or eat leftovers with no complaints. He is my HERO !!!

CONTENT

ACKNOWLEDGMENTS

First and foremost I would like to give honor to God for my life and my creative talent. I would like to thank my mother Alberta Willis-Hicks who introduced me to my love of fabric and recycling very early in my life; that introduction has served me well. I would also like to thank Roland Freeman, author of 'Communion of the Spirits" and Dr. Carolyn Mazloomi, author of 'Spirits of the Cloth', for including me in their books that gave me the beginning of an extensive vehicle that allowed me the ability to share my art quilts with a much broader audience. I would like to acknowledge Sam Gilliam who would take time out of his busy schedule and talk with me about my art whenever Reginald and I would go to Washington DC.

I especially would like to thank my children Angela, Oscar Jr. and Virgil for loving and supporting me as their mom and as an artist. And to the memory of my first born TP, "I am still doing what I love." And last but not least Kyra Hicks for her book 'How to Self Publish Your Own Quilt Catalog', she is a cheerleader for many quilters.

COMMUNITY INFLUENCE......

I have been asked this question many times about "what influence, if any, does your community have on your art/quilt making?"

In life there are some things that you do naturally, without much conscious thought, just because it feels right. Well that is what I do in terms of drawing inspiration from my community. I am from an impoverished area that most people have very few kind words for when they hear the town East St. Louis, IL. But I know the cultural richness and history of the community and that is instrumental in nurturing my creativity. I have never been at a lost to find inspiration, motivation, and visual imagery; many of the youth refer to me as the 'art lady'. I find ways of creating things of beauty from what others see as junk/trash. I do lots of other art creations but with my first love, I recycle old clothing and fabric remnants to create art quilts.

From the beginning.....

I am a life long resident of East St. Louis, IL. I am a graduate of Southern Illinois University at Edwardsville with a Bachelor of Fine Arts and a Masters of Fine Arts degree in Studio Art. I also have a second Masters in Art Therapy. For as long as I can remember I have always wanted to be an artist, even as a child, although I did not know the term artist and what it entailed. But I do remember the warm, comfortable and satisfying feeling that I received every time I did something creative or had creative thoughts. Years later, that satisfying feeling has only magnified. I know that my creative ability is of divine inspiration, because I dream art, I feel art, I get totally excited when I am around art, and through my creations I reveal my internal world.

I facilitate a lot of children's workshops and I enjoy the big smiles on their faces as they complete their designs that they initially said they could not do. They were ready to give up, even before they had tried. I know that not every child want to be an artist, but for those that do I want to be instrumental in aiding them to experience those same types of warm feelings I had as a child whenever I was creative.

Some of my art quilts have been published in numerous books and catalogues, and on a few occasions my art has also been on the cover of books. I know that my creative skills have not yet reached its full development, because I continue to learn daily. I love to experiment with the arts and include found objects, photo transfers, etc., to see what works and what need work. My art quilts have been exhibited in galleries nationally and internationally, and I have been exhibiting my work since the 80's

 Key Facts:

*Multimedia artist

*Workshop facilitator for children as well as adults

*Art exhibitor

*Specialty in creating 'Memory quilts'

*Art Therapist

My fabric art genre is more than 'art quilts'; it's an emotional journey from childhood to the present, filled with wonderful vignettes of memories. I have had a wonderful fascination with fabric for as long as I can remember, dating back to my childhood. It began with me helping my mom recycle our too little or worn out clothing into fabric pieces for a bed quilt. She taught me how to correctly use scissors to remove waistbands from pants and skirts and to square off the fabric sections in preparation for pieces for a future quilt. There was a jar for buttons and a plastic bag for recycled zippers to be used if ever needed. This was also my introduction to early recycling which I do a lot of today. At that time in my life I had no desire to construct a quilt, but I totally enjoyed the de-construction of the clothing. But I do attribute my early de-construction of clothing to my concept of 'memory quilts'. When my siblings and I would cuddle under a quilt in the winter eating toast and oatmeal, we would reminisce about different fabric pieces that we recognized as fabric that had come from a particular piece of clothing.

My mom made quilts by hand because she didn't have a sewing machine, plus she had never learned how to use one. She tried to teach me how to hand sew the sections of fabric together, but I didn't like the constant pricking of my fingers with the needle, and I found it boring at the time and it was too slow of a process. I did however learn to sew in high school and it opened up a whole new world for me. It was fascinating to be able to make my own clothing, as well as re-purpose some of my old items of clothing and give them a new life. And when my grandfather purchased my first sewing machine it was 'heaven'. The machine was mine and I didn't have to share it, and being the oldest of seven children that was great, since there was very little that you didn't have to share in a large household. But the most rewarding was to be able to teach my mom how to use a sewing machine and I did opt to share the machine with her.

It was not until I was an adult, married with four children that I enrolled in college in the Fine arts program, there I learned how to enhance and manipulate my love of fabric with paints, dyes, etc. With the early training with my mom and my high school sewing plus what I learned in college, my love of art quilts began. Although fabric is not my only medium of art, it remains my first love.

I was told early in my art career that I was a storyteller, but of course at that time I never saw it. My designs for my quilts come from dreams, people, music, etc. In essence my ideas come from my every day existence and I am quite passionate about the creative process. Creating is and always will be my 'Zen', my therapeutic bliss.

What does art quilting mean to me......

Art quilts for me mean a multitude of things, first and foremost to me the term "art" means self-expression through the use of whatever medium that I am using at the time. Placing the two words "art" and "quilt" together is a great marriage. I have a great fascination with fabric; I love the way it feels, the many weights of it, and the great color choices as well as the many ways that it can be manipulated and handled. I can paint it, dye it, cut it, tear it, singe it, sew multiple layers together, embellish it, etc., all to create the story or design that I want to portray.

Art quilting to me means total freedom in terms of design, shape and content. One of the things that I think make my work unique is that it is created by me; it is a part of me until I release it. What I find most meaningful in my work and the work of others is the feelings that are evoked by the art.

Whether you like it, or hate it, it creates conversation as to what the creator might have been thinking or feeling at the moment of execution of the art work.

Creating for someone other than myself.....

When I create memory quilts specifically for someone other than myself, I first and foremost want to hear their story, what it is that they are looking for, their thought process, what I can and cannot do, colors they like or dislike, size, shape, etc. Then with that information I use my creativity and my right to edit to take their design from an idea to a reality. I enjoy the give and take in working with an individual. Most of the time they aren't sure what it is they want but they know they want specific items of clothing to be used, such as an old tee-shirt that was a husbands favorite, or a blouse they can no longer wear etc.

I am what I am....

I used to be embarrassed that I was not like other children growing up. I didn't have a sense of self. I wanted to fit in and belong, but I always felt odd and out of sync. But over the years I came to realize that 'I am what I am' a creative being who enjoy the entire process of creativity. I had to grow into embracing being different, now I love my uniqueness, my quirkiness, my way of seeing things, and my way of living. I love the whole thought process that takes place; whereby I get a hint or a clue that could become a potential project. Sometimes I doodle, other times I just hold on to a thought an allow it to undergo incubation. During that thought process I wind and rewind that idea over and over in my head until there is illumination, and this is where the 'light bulb' comes on and it has all been worked out in my head. Other artist may want to work it out in sketches, but for me I like my way better because it works for me. But initially my creative process did present lots of anxiety for me in art school, because of course the instructor couldn't see what was transpiring in my head. Also getting the idea from my head to my hands was not always the easiest. Sometimes I would stumble onto a different creative path once I physically began creating. But that was okay, creating is like life, we start our day with specific plans in mind, but something or someone pulls us off task or in a different direction. I learned early in my creative world to go with the flow, to be flexible, to just let things unfold and to trust my instincts.

I learned to listen to my own inner voice and when I am in the process of creating it is like time is standing still and my soul soars. I am truly a 'soul' that has been royally blessed, I have never wanted to be anything more than what I am and that is an artist. I love revamping, recycling, and reusing things that I have or I find, or I am given. I love trying to find ways of using much of what I have on hand. I very rarely purchase new fabrics, unless it is something in particular that I need. I especially enjoy working with individuals who want to explore their own creativity and to help them find a direction that is suitable and compatible to what they are trying to achieve. I don't want anyone who I work with to be a mini version of myself; I want them to be their own creative being.

A collection of some of my art quilts in one place...

Too many times I have been asked to create a catalog of some of my art quilts, I was never against it; the problem was just taking the time to do it. Making a decision of what to include, what not to include etc. resulted in not doing anything. The time to do a small catalog of my art quilts is now right and emotionally I am just ready. I most certainly want to include art quilts that have been a part of traveling exhibits and/or have had a great impact on me in some way or another, as well as my Obama series, which is extremely important to me. This is a series of seven 'Obama' inspired art quilts, which started with 'Road to Redemption'. I received a call from Dr. Carolyn Mazloomi, art quilter, author and curator, asking if I wanted to participate in a group show.

This exhibit would consist of 44 art quilters who would create art quilts that would be on display in Washington DC for the first African American president, who was also the 44th President of the United States. Of course I wanted to participate and be a part of such an auspicious occasion. And once I committed to the project I had three weeks from start to finish to create and execute a design and mail it to Mr. Roland Freeman, photo-documentarian who spear headed the project. This was a very big undertaking but such a great opportunity. I had a pair of silk draperies that were given to me; I had already prepared the fabric, in terms of removing the hem etc., not knowing that the panels would be used to create a series of art quilts. The idea of a series did not come into play until I had finished that first Obama' quilt.

Stepping outside of my own little world...

The first time I traveled abroad was when I went to Dakar Senegal, West Africa in the early 90's. It was a great experience and it really helped to open me up as an artist. I was stimulated by the people I met, the beauty of the Country, the sounds, smells etc. I have traveled within the States and of course that was always a stimulating experience, but leaving the Country was a bit overwhelming and exciting at the same time.

In 2010 I was blessed to be one of nine artists chosen to create a design that would be replicated into glass murals 5' x 3' and become a permanent installation at the St. Louis Lambert Airport. The completed design was unveiled at the airport in December, 2011 in Concourse A-8. When I first learned that I would be going to Munich Germany, I initially panicked, not outwardly, but internally. It brought back that overwhelming feeling of when I went to West Africa. It was just about my stepping outside of my comfort zone, and not knowing any of the people that I would be traveling with. But it was such a life changing experience and I am glad I did not let my un-comfortable feelings get in the way of my growth as an artist and a person. I have since traveled abroad both in 2011 and 2012, and I see a lot more travel in my future.

I love being an artist, and the thought of living without art would be devastating. I give thanks daily for the talents that I have been blessed with and never want to be without them. Creating for me is like breathing, so necessary for life.

Accomplishments....

I can not state enough that I have never wanted to be anything other than an artist. And by creating my art quilts I satisfy that internal feeling of playing with pieces of fabric as a child and paying attention to the colors, type, weight and texture and finding a way of making them work together. I never created for anyone other than myself, I tried once and it was a failure and I was quite unhappy, so I never did it again. To further elaborate on that, one of my instructors told me specific things to do with a project and against my better judgment I did what was asked of me. Needless to say, during critique at a later time, I was blasted for what I had created, because it seemed forced, which it was! I continue to listen to constructive criticism but I work strongly from my own intuition.

Over the years I have tried to challenge myself in the making of my art because it is so easy to become complacent, and complacent does not wear well.....

One of my great accomplishments is when I created a mosaic turtle that is 7' long and 6' wide and is now on the Southern Illinois University, East St. Louis campus grounds. I took a welding class to create the armature, and a 'concrete form making' class to create the body. Just the thought of taking on such a large endeavor and completing it continues to put a big smile on my face.

Keeping tabs.....

I have created a large quantity of art quilts, so many that it is difficult to have an accurate count in my head, but I have kept images on disc as well as photo images and slides. It is always amazing when I periodically look at all of the work that I have created over the years. I love not just creating art quilts but art in general, I love recycling, re-purposing, and up-cycling objects and furniture pieces that have been discarded by others. I tie it all to my love of quilting and patch work in terms of the way I lay out and execute my designs.

One of my goals is to continue on a grander scale to do both children and adult workshops. I enjoy combining both my art therapy skills, my fine art skills and my intuition to create unique creative workshops that are both informative, and relaxing.

Studio space- one place or many....

I have a specific place in my home where my sewing machines, fabric, and many other creative tools are housed or contained, but my entire home is my studio. Many friends, family members as well as some community family look for opportunities to come to my home to see the latest things I have been working on both inside and outside our home (I like making yard art). I create out of an internal need as a result of many of life's trials and tribulations. Art has always been my saving grace. Whenever I have wanted to submit to defeat and become swallowed up by 'darkness', my art always gave me the drive that I needed to pull myself through. For me, art is more than creating works of art, it is my purpose, it is my grace, and it is my gift.

How I would like to be remembered as an artist....

My art has given me courage to grow, and it has allowed me a voice when words were too deep to release. My art has helped me to bridge many gaps in my life. It brings me great joy, and I hope that is also touches the lives of others. I would love to be remembered as: 'Edna J. Patterson-Petty, a warm and loving spirit who lived to create and created to live.'

The 'Obama' series......

There are seven art quilts in this series created from 2008-2010. Normally I choose not to work in a series, but this was so important to me. After creating the first art quilt 'Road to Redemption' I felt that I had more to say, more to express, because there were a lot of African Americans that made it possible for Obama to become the first African American President.

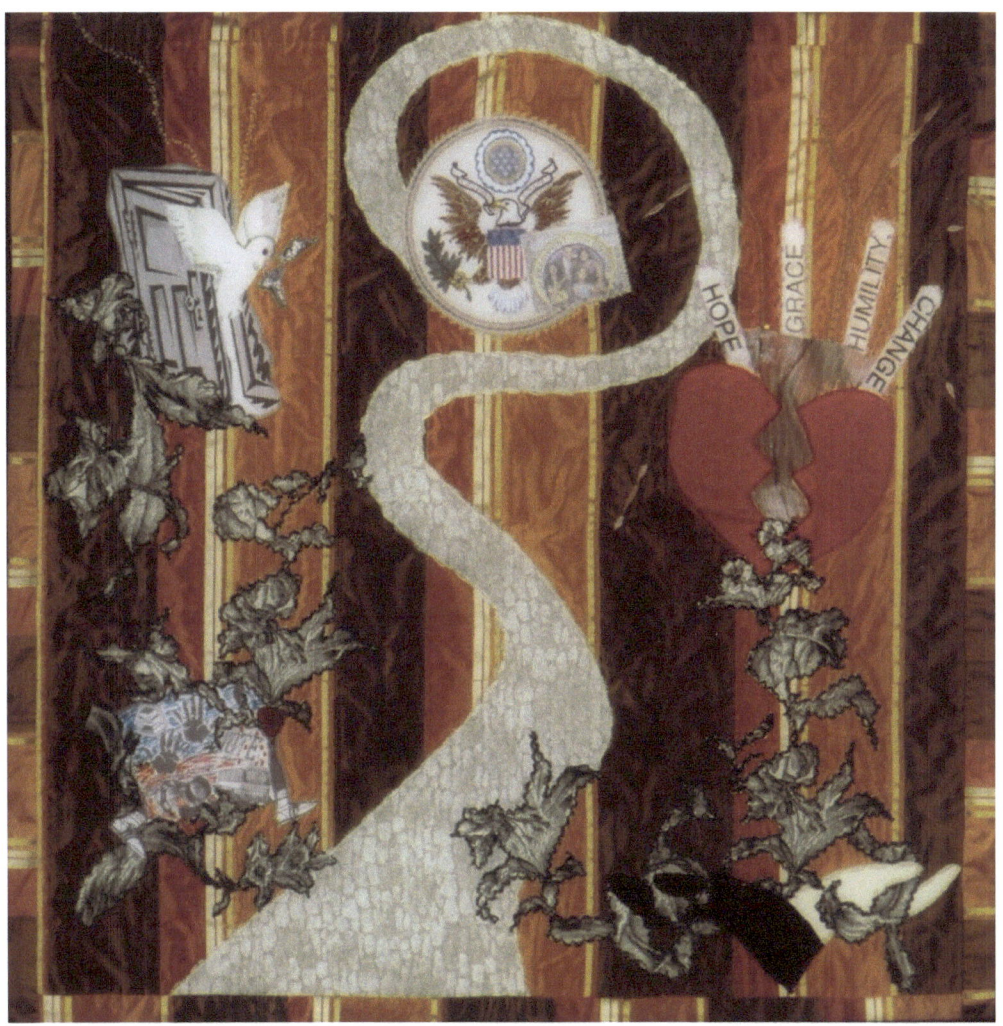

©Road to Redemption 36 x 36, 2008, owner Missouri Historical Society
(*Inspired by Bob Marley's music 'Redemption Song'*

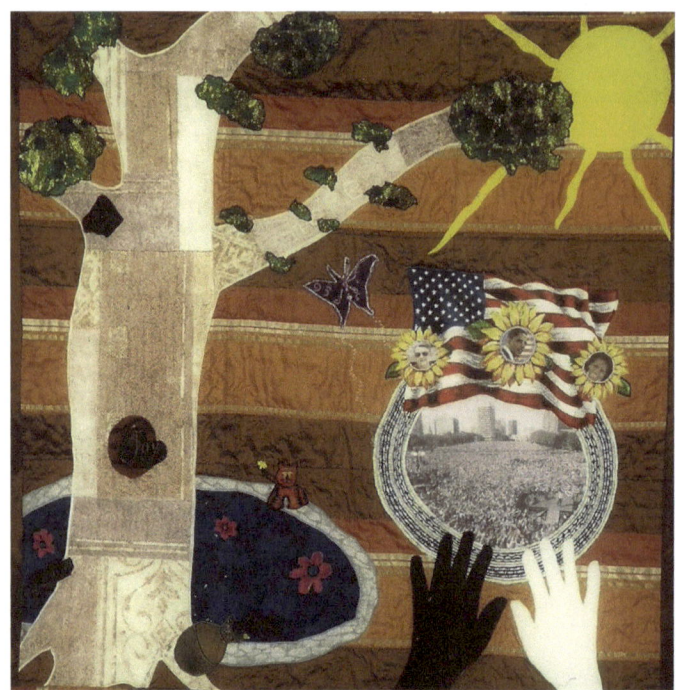

©A Clear and Sunny Day, 36 x 36, 2008, owner Rhonda Daniels
This was inspired by Obama's trip to St. Louis, Mo.

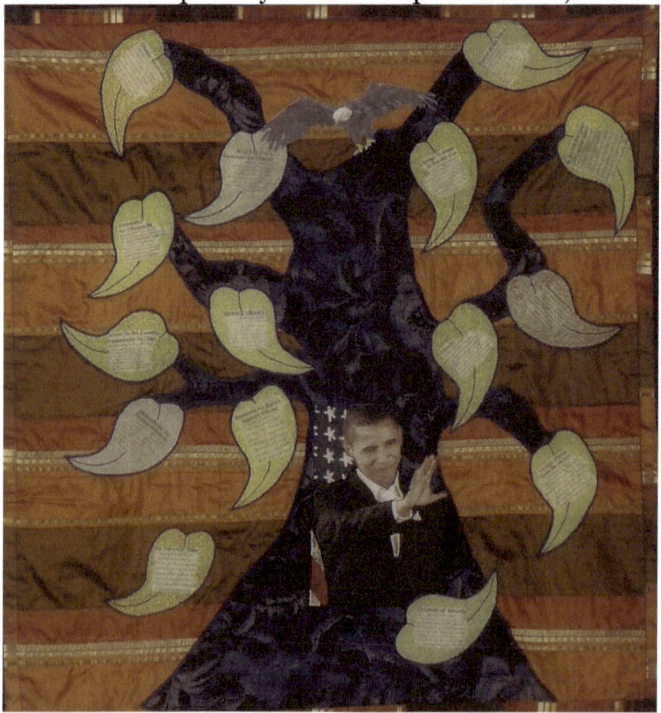

©The Royal Kwansaba Tree, 36x 36, 2009, owner Charlois Lumpkin
Inspired by Eugene Redmond's' writers group

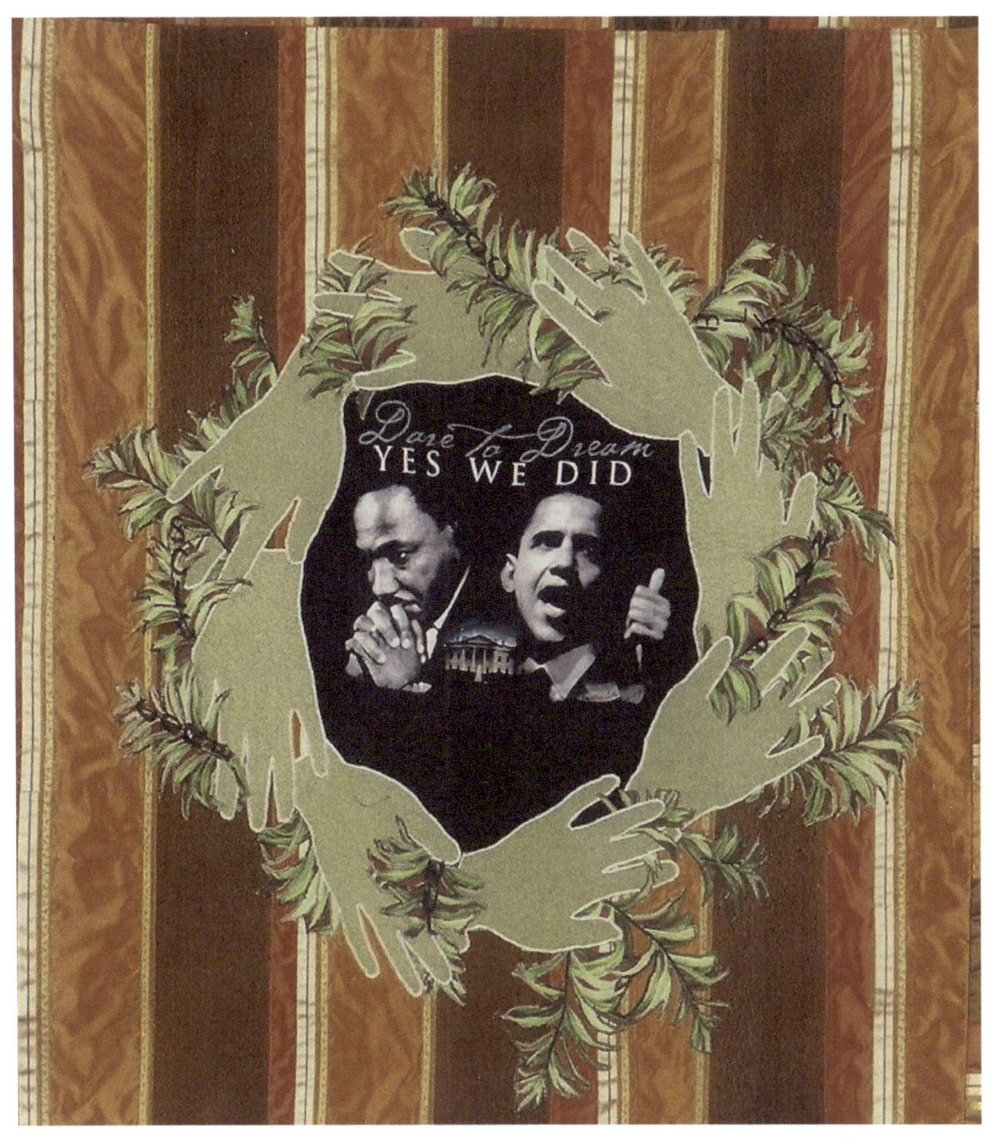

©Forty-Forty-Four, 36 x 36, 2009, anonymous donor
Purchased for school district #189 East St. Louis

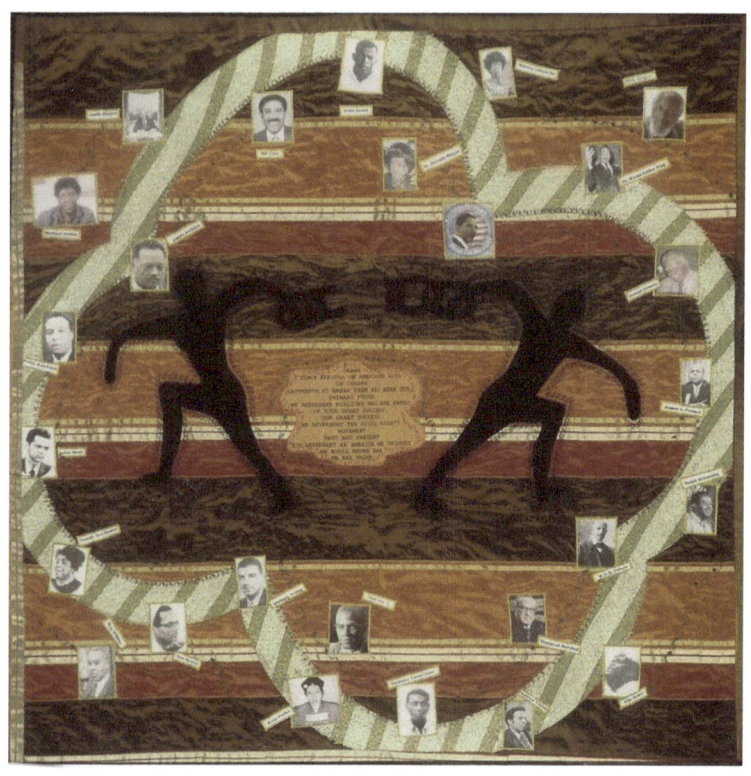

© Breaking Down Barriers, 36 x 36, 2010, owners Erin & Mark Kern Breaking down barriers was inspired by the many people that made it possible for Obama to become the first African American president of the U.S.A (by no means is this all of the people, but this is 23 of the people that are prominent in our history. *The words in the center of the quilt were written by my husband Reginald Petty.*

Breaking down barriers
Since arrival on American soil in chains, attempts to break them have been our primary focus. We represent millions who are proud of your success, our success. We represent the Civil Rights movement past and present. You represent and America we thought we would never see. We are proud!!!

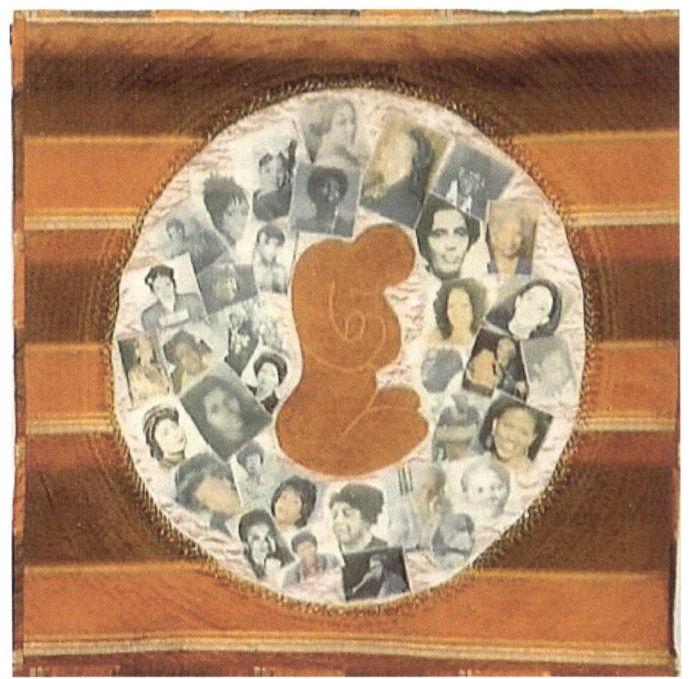

©If it Weren't for the Women, 36 x35, 2010

This quilt was inspired the important roles that women play in all of life,
one of the women is my grandmother.

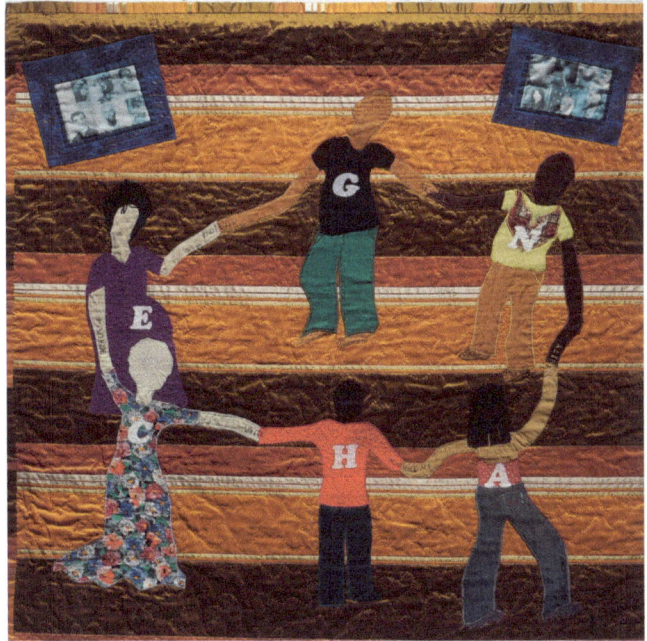

©Change, 36 x36, 2010

This is the last of the Obama series, and it was inspired by his inspiration
to both young and old and how his belief system impacts us all.

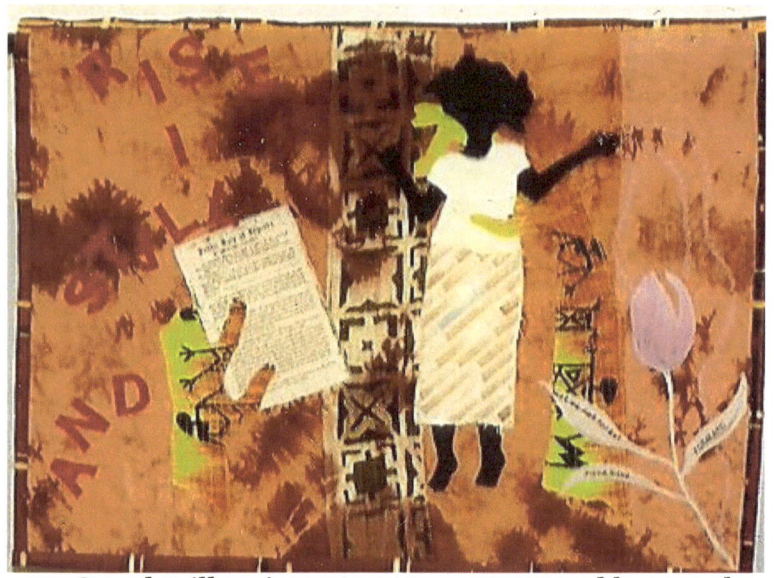

©And Still I Rise, 28 x 66, 2011, owned by Angela Robertson

'And still I Rise' was inspired by the public notice about women being sold. I found the notice on line, and once I checked to make sure I could use it, the ideas began.

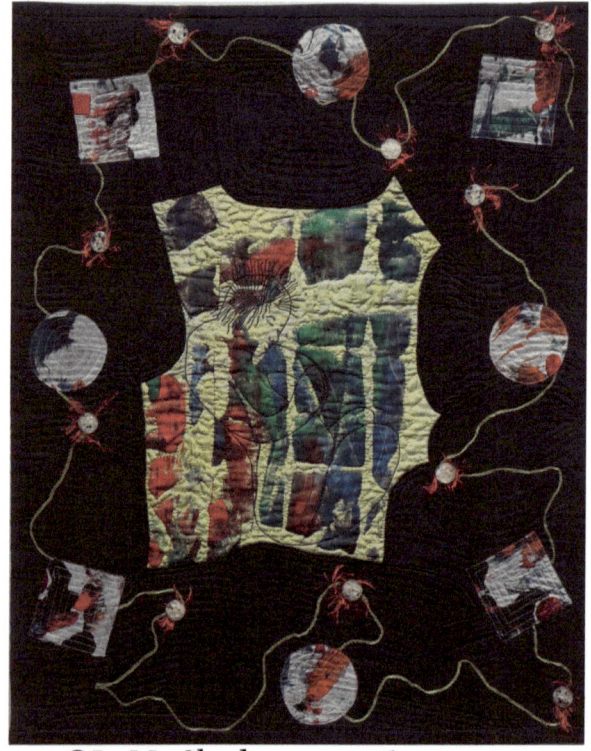

©In My Shadow, 29x 36, 2011

Inspired by some women's struggle with insecurities

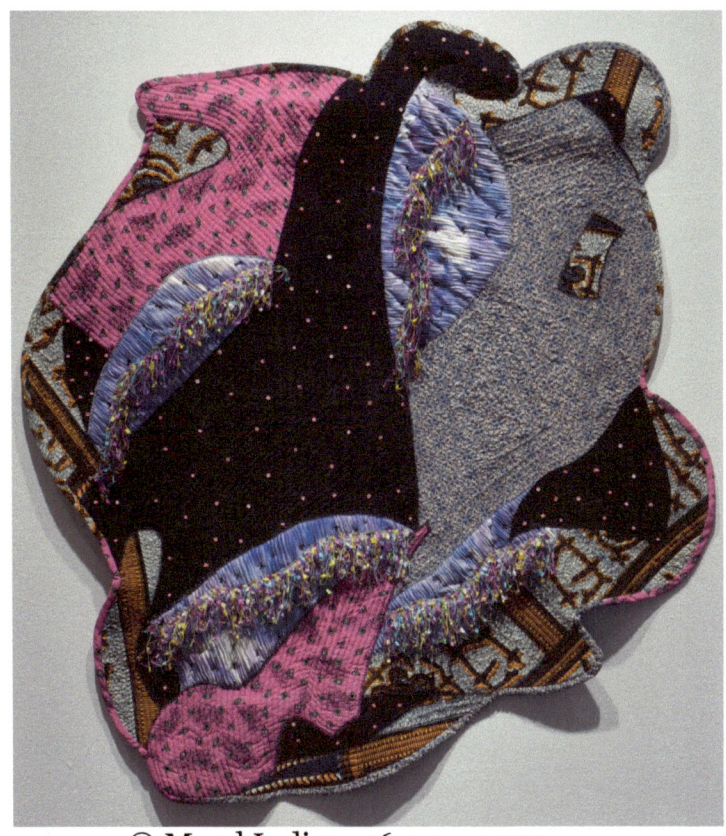

© Mood Indigo, 46 x 32, 2005
The inspiration came from listing to the song of the same title by Duke Ellington
and I let the music dictate the design as well as the contents of the piece

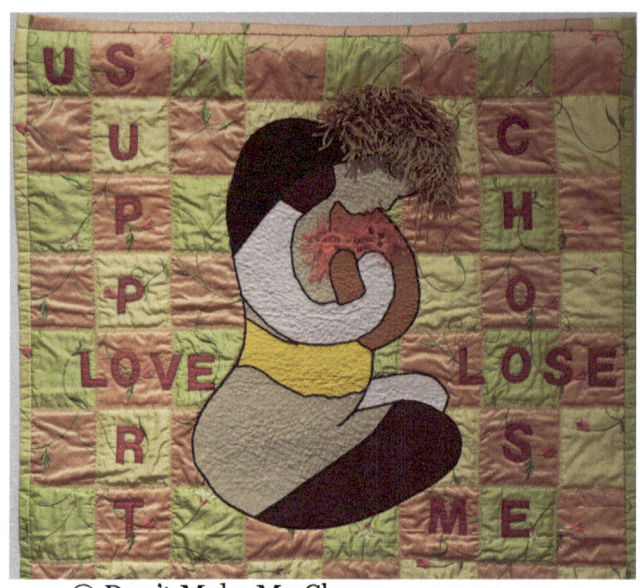

© Don't Make Me Choose, 32 x 35, 2009
I was inspired by the documentary 'Who does She think She Is'

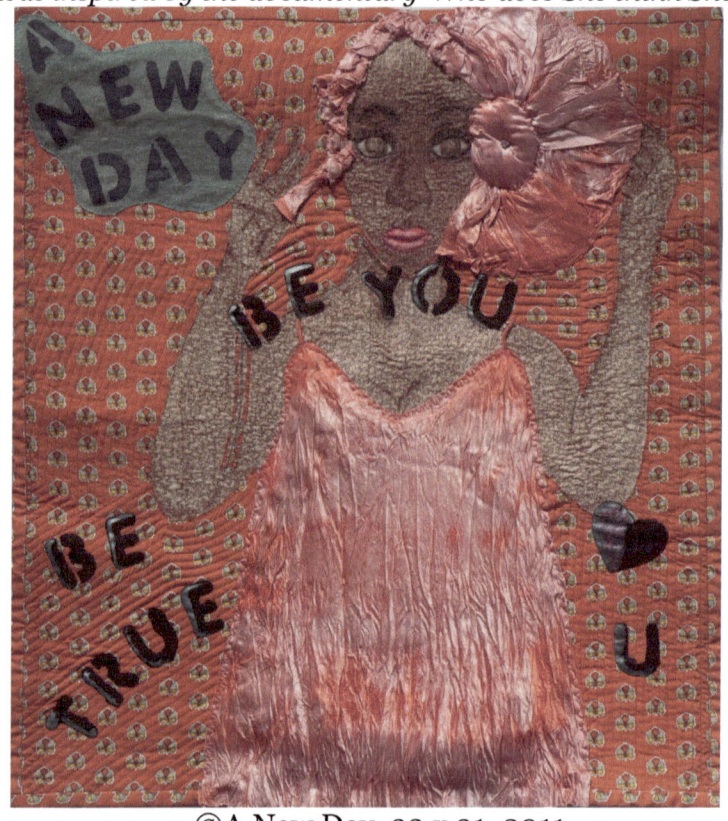

©A New Day, 33 x 31, 2011,
As a therapist, I have worked with a lot of young women trying to package themselves for that man in their lives.

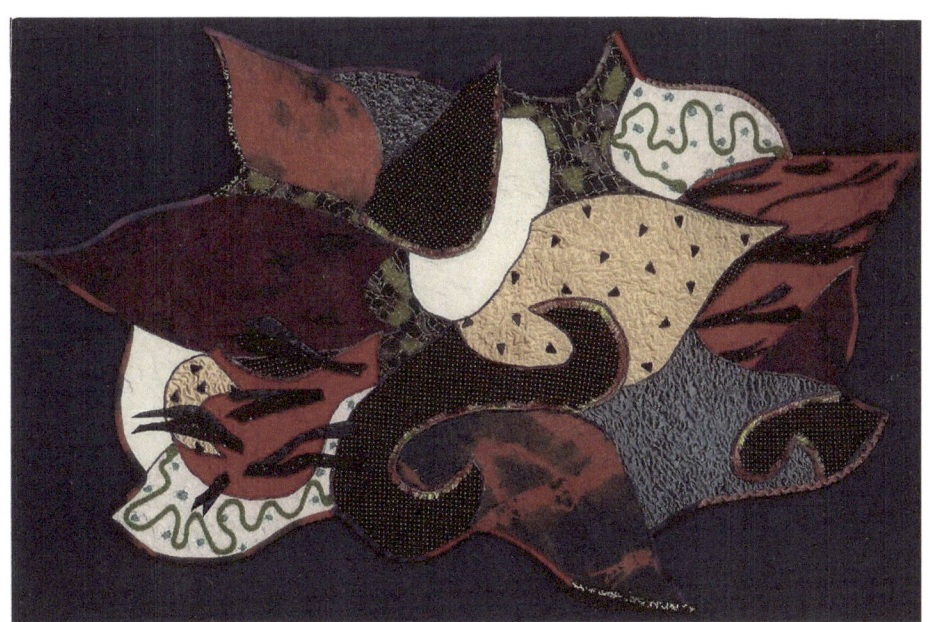

©Do You Feel Me, 57 x 36, private owner,
Inspired by song of the same title.

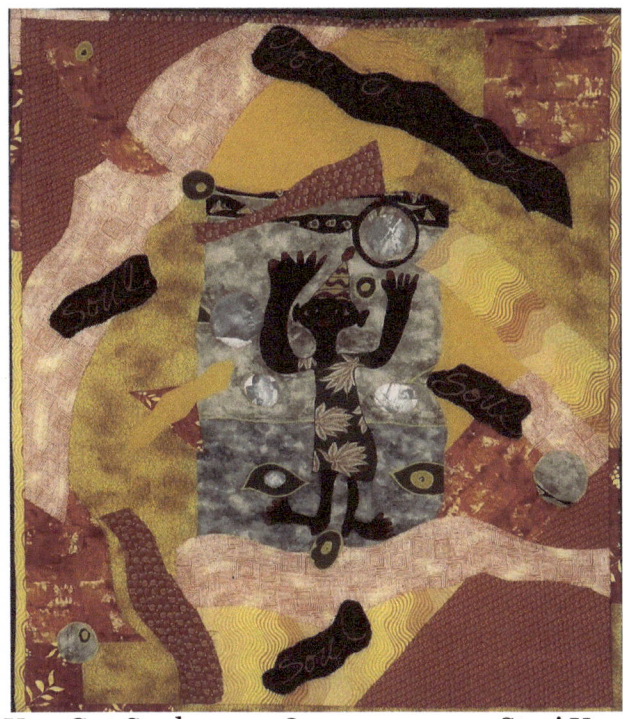

© You Got Soul, 42 x 38, 2005, owner Staci Yandle
Inspired by members of East St. Louis, jazz band.

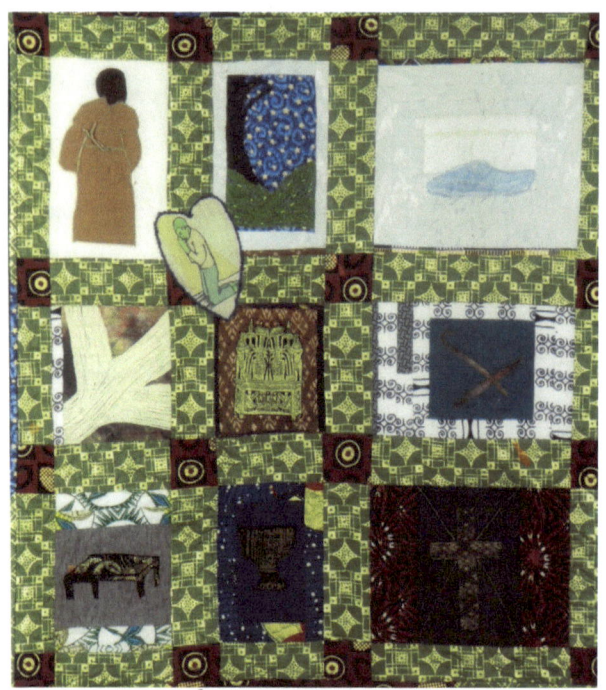

©23rd Pslam46 x 41, 2003
Inspired by a dream

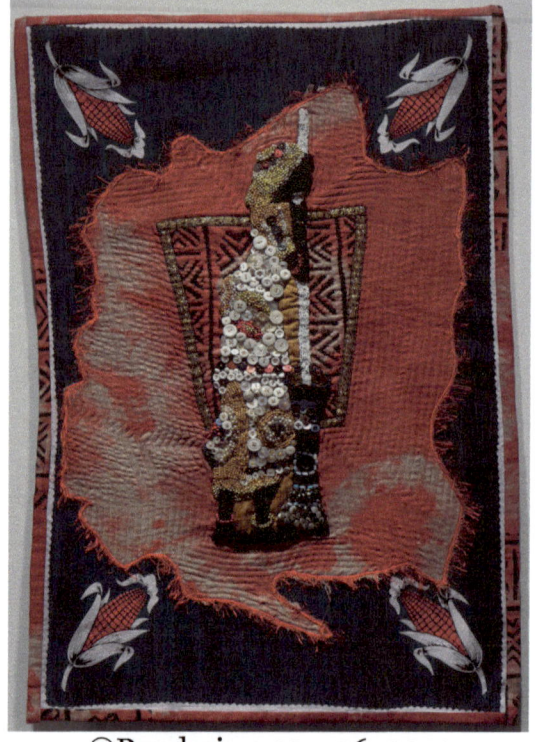

©Pondering 40 x 26, 2011
Inspired by life challenges

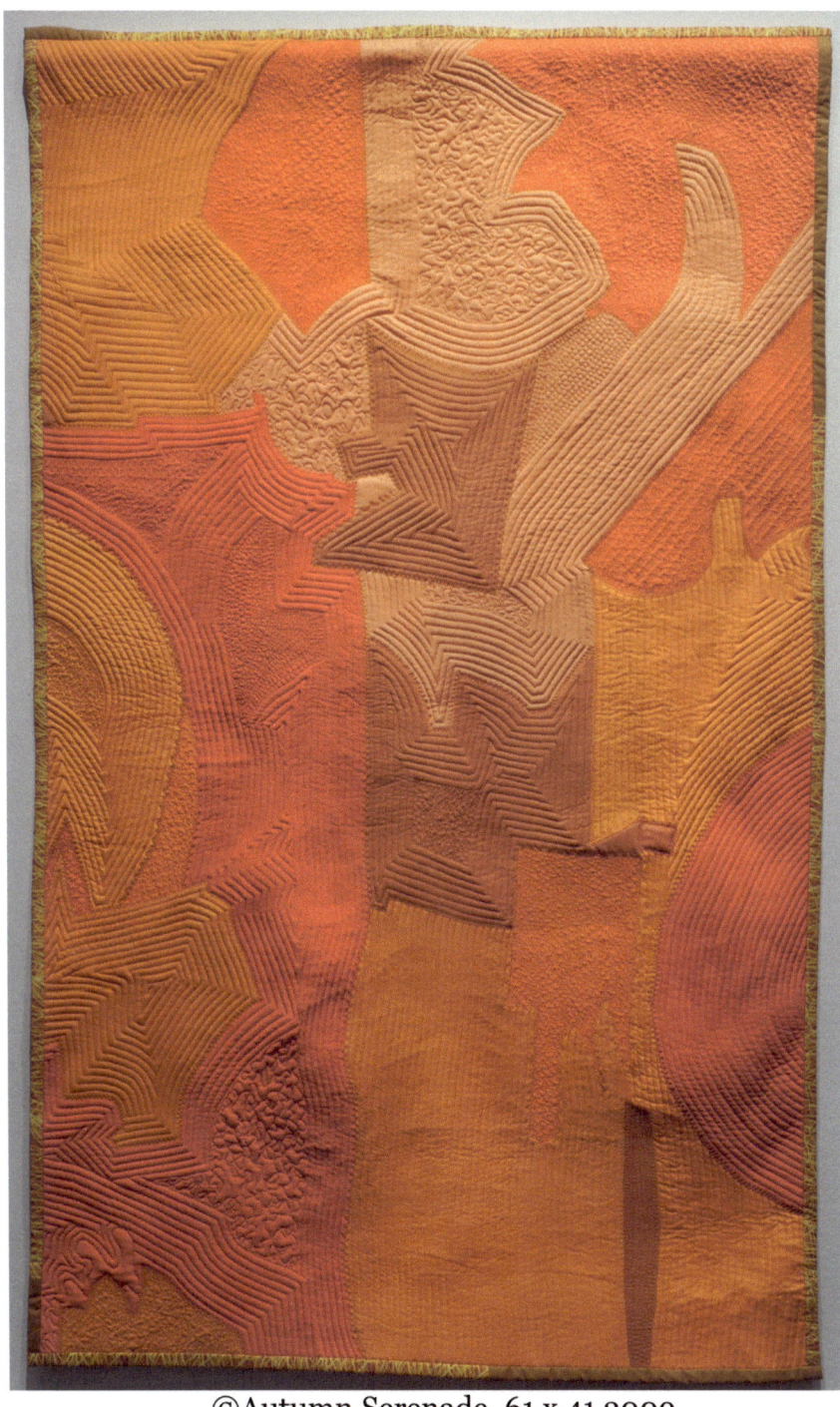

©Autumn Serenade, 61 x 41 2009

The inspiration for this quilt came from a box of scraps that I was given and each piece on the quilt was not altered in shape. The instrumental 'Autumn Serenade' was playing in the background.

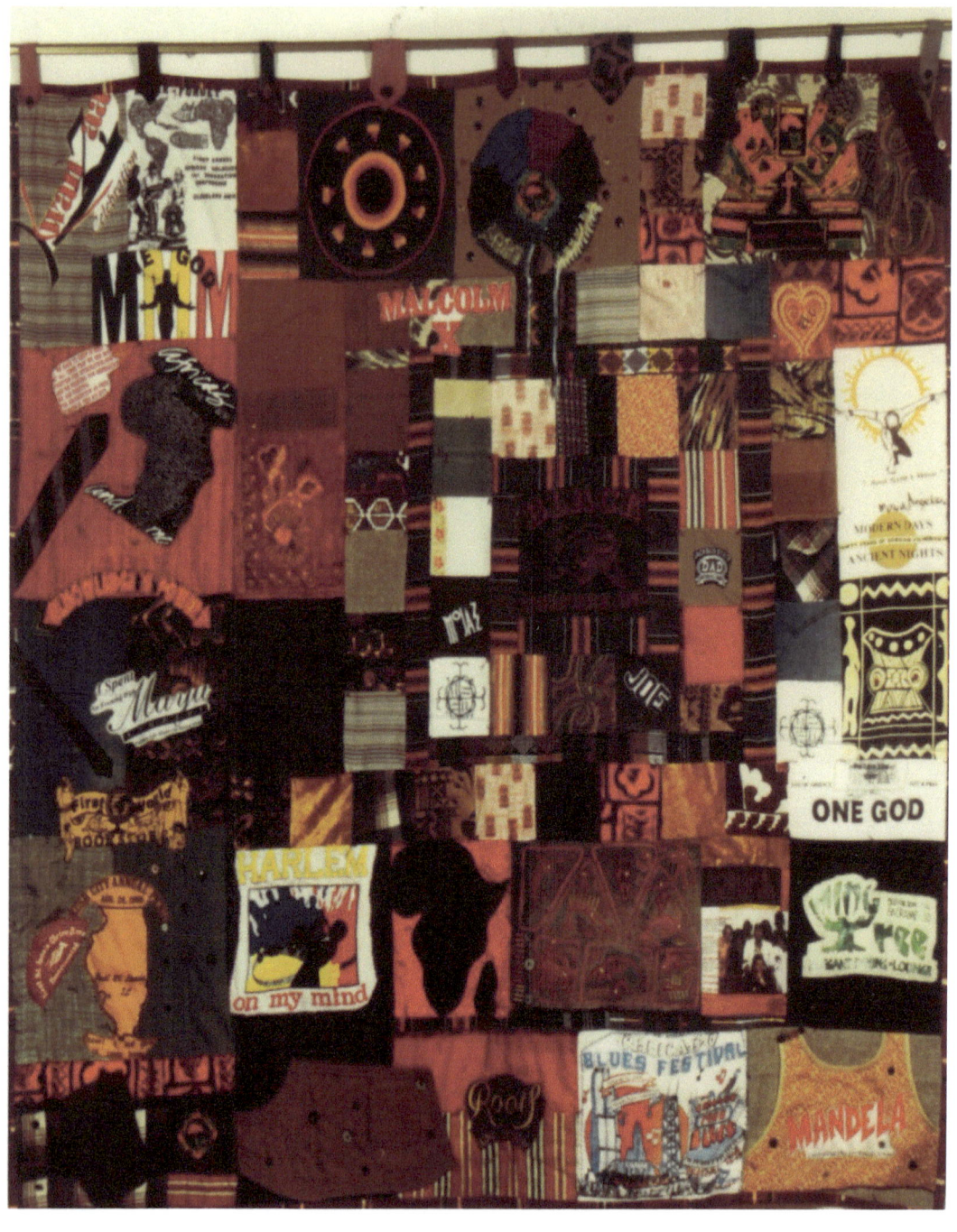

©Redmond's Memories, 80 x 80, 1998

This art quilt represented 40 years of Professor Eugene Redmond's life at

the time that it was created.

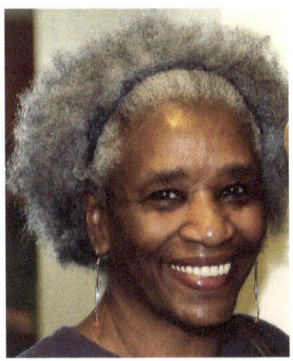

Edna J. Patterson-Petty

Multi-media Fabric Artist\Art Therapist

East St. Louis, IL. 62204

ebonygirlp@aol.com

Patterson-Petty holds a Masters of Fine Arts degree in Studio Art. She also holds a Masters degree in Art Therapy. Both degrees received from SIU-E, at Edwardsville, IL. Patterson-Petty presently lives in East St. Louis, where she was reared, with her husband Reginald Petty. She presently works as a practicing artist as well as an Art Therapist. Mrs. Patterson-Petty has exhibited her works of art in numerous galleries, museums, and universities. Her works also hang in many homes across the country. Some of her works are published in *Communion of the Spirit, by Roland Freeman, and Spirits of the Cloth, by Carolyn Mazloomi, United States Embassy-Islamabad, Art in Embassies Program, Fabric Art Gallery, by Leisure Arts Publication, Portfolio 12, 13'14,by Studio Art Quilts Association, SIU-E Alumnus, Port of Harlem: magazine about Blacks at Home & Abroad, and this year had works published on two covers of the African American Revue, published by SLU, and The American Art Therapy Journal, Textural Rhythms: Quilting the Jazz Tradition, and Quilting African American Women's History by Carolyn Mazloomi.* Edna was also inducted into the College of Arts & Sciences, SIU Alumni Hall of Fame, in 2009.

Edna stated that she always thought that her success in the arts, whatever that entailed, depended on others. She constantly looked for validation outside of herself.

She finally came to the conclusion that more than anything, "you must have faith in who, and what you are and continue to hone your talents, have faith, and give self validation and more than anything listen to the voice of her own heart". Thereby bringing balance to her life.

Patterson-Petty has also stepped into the realm of public art, she has a welcome mat design designed in terrazzo stone of one of her art quilts at a metro-link stop in Washington Park, IL., and a permanent glass mural that depicts one of her designs, at St. Louis Lambert Airport, and a large mosaic turtle design (7' x 6') on East St. Louis campus of Southern Illinois University.

www.ingramcontent.com/pod-product-compliance
Lightning Source LLC
Chambersburg PA
CBHW041306180526
45172CB00003B/995